CAT-ECHISMS

CAT-ECHISMS

FUNDAMENTALS

OF

FELINE FAITH

ELLIS WEINER AND BARBARA DAVILMAN

PHOTOGRAPHS BY SUSAN BURNSTINE

ST. MARTIN'S GRIFFIN

NEW YORK

CAT-ECHISMS. Copyright © 2010 by Ellis Weiner and Barbara
Davilman. All rights reserved. Printed in the United States of
America. For information, address St. Martin's Press,
175 Fifth Avenue, New York, N.Y. 10010.

www.stmartins.com

Library of Congress Cataloging-in-Publication Data

Weiner, Ellis.
    Cat-echisms : fundamentals of feline faith / Ellis Weiner
and Barbara Davilman ; photographs by Susan Burnstine.—1st ed.
        p. cm.
    ISBN 978-0-312-59616-3
    1. Cats—Humor.   I. Davilman, Barbara.   II. Title.
    PN6231.C23W45 2010
    818'.5402—dc22

                                        2009040018

            10   9   8   7   6   5   4   3   2

TO LAURIE WINER (SHE KNOWS WHY)

AND THE CAT PEOPLE

CONTENTS

ACKNOWLEDGMENTS   xi

INTRODUCTION   1

1. LESSON THE FIRST: ON THE DIVINITY
AND QUASI-DIVINITY OF CATS   3

2. LESSON THE SECOND: ON THE BEHAVIORS
AND DISPOSITIONS OF CATS   31

3. LESSON THE THIRD: ON THE RELATIONSHIP BETWEEN CATS
AND OTHER ANIMALS, NOT EXCLUDING DOGS   65

4. LESSON THE FOURTH: ON THE RELATIONSHIP
BETWEEN CATS AND HUMANS   79

ACKNOWLEDGMENTS

Many thanks to the Lange Foundation (www.lange foundation.com) for their heroic rescue work with cats and dogs, and to Salli Sammut for her hand-holding and assistance.

CAT-ECHISMS

INTRODUCTION

Q. What is the Catechism?

A. *The Catechism is a series of lessons, in question-and-answer form, outlining the fundamental beliefs and principles of the Catholic church.*

Q. What is *Cat-echisms*?

A. *Cat-echisms is our latest book; it mimics the style of the Catechism but is strictly about cats.*

Q. We thought you only wrote about dogs.

A. *You must re-state that in the form of a question.*

Q. Don't you only write about dogs?

A. *We frequently do write about dogs, as in the precursor to this book, which is entitled* Arffimations: Meditations for Your Dog.

Q. So, okay, but wait—are you saying that all cats are Catholic?

A. *We are not saying that all cats are Catholic. In fact no cats are Catholic. The religion of cats is a form of autotheism, which is a term we just made up to mean cats worship themselves.*

Q. If cats worship themselves, where do humans fit in?

A. *You will see where and how humans fit in after reading this book. Please proceed.*

1.

LESSON THE FIRST

ON THE DIVINITY

AND QUASI-DIVINITY

OF CATS

ON THE DIVINITY AND QUASI-DIVINITY OF CATS

I AM NOT HERE TO AMUSE YOU

Q. Are you here to amuse humans?

A. *I am not here to amuse humans.*

Q. Then why do you exist?

A. *I exist to cause sniffling, sneezing, wheezing, and hives to humans who are allergic to my sacred dander.*

Q. Why is your dander sacred?

A. *My dander is sacred because it consists of dead flakes of my precious skin and dried bits of my divine saliva.*

Q. What if I'm not allergic?

A. *Then you are free to worship me.*

ON THE DIVINITY AND QUASI-DIVINITY OF CATS

CAUSES AND CONSEQUENCES
OF MY DIVINE SENSE OF FOCUS

Q. How are you able to achieve your divine sense
of focus?

A. *I am able to achieve my divine sense of focus
because my species has deliberately determined to
perfect our ability to focus.*

Q. Why is it important to be able to focus?

A. *It is important because without it we become
distracted, and never achieve or accomplish
anything. We are a very results-oriented species.
That is why we still exist after thousands of years.*

Q.

A. *You're not listening to me, are you?*

Q. Sorry, I just got a text.

ON THE DIVINITY AND QUASI-DIVINITY OF CATS

GODLINESS IS NEXT TO CLEANLINESS

Q. Why does licking your paw resemble the act of prayer?

A. *Licking your paw resembles the act of prayer because you lick your paw to tidy up the outer cat, and you pray to tidy up the inner cat.*

Q. What part of the outer cat needs tidying up?

A. *All of it.*

Q. What part of the inner cat needs tidying up?

A. *You don't want to know.*

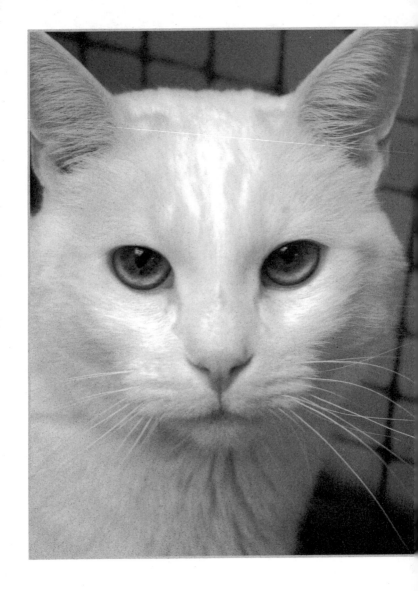

ON THE DIVINITY AND QUASI-DIVINITY OF CATS

GORGEOUS IN THE SWEDISH MANNER

Q. Who is gorgeous?

A. *I am gorgeous.*

Q. How are you gorgeous?

A. *I am gorgeous in the Swedish manner.*

Q. Why is your manner of gorgeousness particularly Swedish?

A. *Because I am a striking blonde with dazzling blue eyes.*

Q. Does this make you superior to all other cats?

A. *This makes me superior to all other cats, dogs, birds, fish, humans, flowers, and all fruits except pomegranates.*

ON THE DIVINITY AND QUASI-DIVINITY OF CATS

I AM DESCENDED FROM GODS

Q. From what gods are you descended?

A. *I am descended from the cat-god Bast, the local deity of Bubastis, who was worshipped by the ancient Egyptians.*

Q. Why did the ancient Egyptians worship cats?

A. *The ancient Egyptians worshipped cats because cats protected their grain from vermin, and cats were able to kill snakes such as cobras, and because cats were, even in ancient times, totally fabulous.*

Q. How can mankind today show cats the respect they were shown in ancient Egypt?

A. *They can start by doing the same thing the ancient Egyptians did when their cat died.*

Q. What did they do?

A. *They shaved their eyebrows and mummified the cat. They did this in the city of Bubastis, but you can have it done in your own local city or town.*

ON THE DIVINITY AND QUASI-DIVINITY OF CATS

I PROUDLY EMBODY THE FIVE KINDS
OF ADORABLENESS

Q. What are the Five Kinds of Adorableness?

A. *The Five Kinds of Adorableness are:*

    a. Adorableness of Eyes

    b. Adorableness of Face

    c. Adorableness of Expression

    d. Adorableness of Body

    e. Adorableness of Being Totally
       Freaking Adorable

Q. What is the difference between saying one is adorable and saying one is cute?

A. *"You are cute" is what you say to cats who aren't adorable, so as not to hurt their feelings. Isn't that adorable?*

ON THE DIVINITY AND QUASI-DIVINITY OF CATS

THE OBJECT OF MY CONTEMPLATION

Q. What is the object of your contemplation?

A. *The object of my contemplation is a cobweb in the corner of the ceiling.*

Q. There is a cobweb in the corner of the ceiling?

A. *Yes.*

Q. How long has it been there?

A. *Long enough that you should fire your cleaning person.*

ON THE DIVINITY AND QUASI-DIVINITY OF CATS

I AM DEVOUT IN MY RELIGION OF STILLNESS

Q. What do you worship in your religion of stillness?

A. *In my religion of stillness I worship being very, very still, and not moving unless it is absolutely necessary, not doing very much of anything, and just lying around.*

Q. Is that the same thing as being lazy?

A. *No.*

Q. Why is it not the same thing as being lazy?

A. *Because it's a religion.*

ON THE DIVINITY AND QUASI-DIVINITY OF CATS

ON THE PERFECTION OF MY COMPOSURE

Q. How are you able to maintain such perfect composure?

A. *I am able to maintain such perfect composure because I do not fear death.*

Q. Why do you not fear death?

A. *I do not fear death because I possess nine lives.*

Q. Why do you believe God gave you nine lives?

A. *God gave us nine lives to prove to dogs that He likes us better.*

ON THE DIVINITY AND QUASI-DIVINITY OF CATS

THERE IS A LESSON IN MY PROFILE

Q. Why do you look up into the tree?

A. *I look up into the tree so you can see the perfection of my profile.*

Q. What does one gain from seeing the perfection of your profile?

A. *One is reminded that life has many sides.*

Q. What is the benefit of learning that life has many sides?

A. *The benefit is that one becomes a much more open human being; one attracts many different kinds of new experiences into one's life, participates in these experiences, and, in so doing, forgets about me and leaves me free to get that squirrel I have my eye on.*

ON THE DIVINITY AND QUASI-DIVINITY OF CATS

THIS IS NOT "PLAY"

Q. What are you doing?

A. *I am swatting and batting around this little thingie at the end of this cord.*

Q. Is this not "play"?

A. *This is not "play."*

Q. If it is not "play," what is it?

A. *It is a spiritual practice.*

Q. What is spiritual about swatting and batting around a little thingie at the end of a cord?

A. *What is spiritual about drinking wine and eating crackers? Or sitting in a room and singing? It is because we say it is.*

Q. Do you also swat and bat around electrical cords?

A. *No. I do not recognize the spiritual legitimacy of electrical cords. I'm Orthodox.*

ON THE DIVINITY AND QUASI-DIVINITY OF CATS

THE IMPORTANCE OF BEING FLUFFY

Q. What is important about being fluffy?

A. *Being fluffy marks one as a superior creature.*

Q. Aren't all cats fluffy?

A. *Not all cats are fluffy. Only the superior ones.*

Q. Is it the fluffiness that makes the cat superior?

A. *Why not? Isn't that enough?*

ON THE DIVINITY AND QUASI-DIVINITY OF CATS

TO STARE AT NOTHING IS TO LOOK WITHIN

Q. Why do you stare at nothing?

A. *I do not stare at nothing, but only at things you cannot see.*

Q. What do you stare at that we cannot see?

A. *I stare at the great blank timeless void of the Cat Overmind.*

Q. What is the nature of the great blank timeless void of the Cat Overmind?

A. *Its nature is one of greatness, blankness, timelessness, and supreme consciousness of Clear-Minded Thought-Free Empty-Headed Vacuum-Brained Infinitely-No-One-Home-Upstairs Nothingness.*

Q. What is the benefit of experiencing such a state?

A. *When I return from such a state, everything else, including myself, is fascinating. Especially myself.*

2.

LESSON THE SECOND

ON THE BEHAVIORS

AND DISPOSITIONS

OF CATS

ON THE BEHAVIORS AND DISPOSITIONS OF CATS

DO NOT DISTURB

Q. Why do you lie with your head upside-down?

A. *I lie with my head upside-down to let the world know I am officially off-duty and I am not to be disturbed.*

Q. What do you do when you are on-duty?

A. *I lie on newspapers, magazines, and homework; I stare at the wall; I wiggle my butt before pouncing on birds.*

Q. Is that all?

A. *That is all I will discuss at present. I am off-duty.*

ON THE BEHAVIORS AND DISPOSITIONS OF CATS

SACRIFICES OF BEING A MOM

Q. Are these your kittens?

A. *No, these are not my kittens, I'm watching them for a friend. OF COURSE THESE ARE MY KITTENS.*

Q. Why are you shouting? Are you still hormonal?

A. *OF COURSE I'M STILL HORMONAL.*

Q. Do you like being a mom?

A. *I like being a mom but I am sad to have to put my career on hold.*

ON THE BEHAVIORS AND DISPOSITIONS OF CATS

DO NOT APPROACH ME AT THIS TIME

Q. Why should one not approach you at this time?

A. *One should not approach me because I am eating.*

Q. When else should one not approach you?

A. *One should not approach me when I am sleeping, playing in a paper bag, sitting quietly and blinking, or walking around thinking about air.*

Q. When, then, may one approach you?

A. *At eleven-thirty in the morning on Tuesdays and Fridays.*

ON THE BEHAVIORS AND DISPOSITIONS OF CATS

DO NOT TEST MY FEROCITY

Q. What do you mean, do not test your ferocity?

A. *I mean, do not provoke me to see if I am capable of being ferocious, because I am.*

Q. What causes you to become ferocious?

A. *Birds. Mice. Certain grasshoppers. That little thingie that you wave around. And the tassel at the end of the whosis on the doohickey by the lamp. I hate that.*

ON THE BEHAVIORS AND DISPOSITIONS OF CATS

HOW SPLENDID, TO BE THE CAT OF MANY COLORS

Q. Why is it splendid to be the cat of many colors?

A. *It is splendid to be the cat of many colors because my lineage is visible for all to see upon my body and my face.*

Q. What does your lineage consist of?

A. *My lineage consists of a jillion previous cats going back millennia, to ancient Egypt.*

Q. How has your physical form evolved over that time?

A. *It hasn't. Unlike humans, who are descended from apes and did have to evolve, cats have only had to evolve emotionally and spiritually.*

Q. Have you evolved emotionally and spiritually?

A. *I'm still talking to you, am I not?*

ON THE BEHAVIORS AND DISPOSITIONS OF CATS

DON'T LOOK NOW, BUT
I AM A MASTER POUNCER

Q. Why do you survey the floor below?

A. *I survey the floor below so I can be ready to pounce!*

Q. What things will you pounce upon?

A. *I will pounce upon mice, certain balls of yarn, a piece of paper stuck to the end of a wire that waves around like a moth, and the little red light emitted by a laser pointer.*

Q. Why will you pounce on these items?

A. *Because it is my mission in life.*

Q. What will you do once you have pounced on them?

A. *I will lose interest and wander off.*

Q. Why will you lose interest and wander off?

A. *Because that is my other mission in life.*

ON THE BEHAVIORS AND DISPOSITIONS OF CATS

I AM NEVER MORE ALIVE THAN WHEN I SLEEP

Q. Why are you never more alive than when you sleep?

A. *I am never more alive than when I sleep because the state of sleep is the highest expression of felinity, or of being a cat.*

Q. Really?

A. *Yes. Because being asleep embodies:*

    a. silence
    b. stillness
    c. mysteriousness
    d. cuteness
    e. being asleep

ON THE BEHAVIORS AND DISPOSITIONS OF CATS

MY TONGUE IS ROUGH LIKE SANDPAPER
FOR A REASON

Q. Why is your tongue rough like sandpaper?

A. *My tongue is rough like sandpaper so that when I groom myself by licking I am able to harvest the maximum amount of hairs and impurities.*

Q. Why is it important to harvest the maximum amount of hairs and impurities?

A. *To be really clean! And also to create a hairball as big and dense and horrible as possible.*

Q. Why is it important to create a big, dense, horrible hairball?

A. *So that after I cough it up and leave the room, people will know I was there.*

ON THE BEHAVIORS AND DISPOSITIONS OF CATS

I LOOK WITHIN

Q. Why do you close your eyes but keep your head up?

A. *I close my eyes but keep my head up because sometimes I look within to determine what my needs are.*

Q. What are your needs?

A. *At the present time my needs include the need to move some of my toys around in an arbitrary manner, the need to torment the dog, and the need to stare enigmatically at a chair.*

Q. How do you determine which of these needs should be satisfied?

A. *I determine this by looking within and then doing whatever the hell I want.*

ON THE BEHAVIORS AND DISPOSITIONS OF CATS

I CAN SIT IN TREES

Q. Why is it important that you can sit in trees?

A. *It is not important.*

Q. When you sit in trees, do y—wait. What? Did you say it is not important?

A. *I said it is not important.*

Q. Then why do you bring it up?

A. *I bring it up to control the conversation. It's what I do.*

Q. Why—

A. *It's what I do.*

Q. W—

A. *I control the conversation.*

ON THE BEHAVIORS AND DISPOSITIONS OF CATS

MY FAITH IN MY OWN COOLNESS IS UNSHAKEABLE

Q. Why is your faith in your own coolness unshakeable?

A. *My faith in my own coolness is unshakeable because I remain detached and calm no matter what happens.*

Q. Why is it good to remain detached and calm no matter what happens?

A. *It is good because that is how one retains one's dignity in all situations.*

Q. Is there a name for a cat who fails to maintain his or her dignity in all situations?

A. *Yes, there is. That kind of cat is known as a dog.*

ON THE BEHAVIORS AND DISPOSITIONS OF CATS

ON THE PURPOSE OF CHEWING ONE'S FOOT

Q. What is the purpose of chewing one's foot?

A. *The purpose of chewing one's foot is to clean between the toes.*

Q. Is it a sacred ritual with an ancient and arcane history, an act of spiritual discipline comparable to the positions of Hatha Yoga or the spinning of Sufi dervishes?

A. *No. It's how we wash our feet.*

Q. But is—

A. *Just stop.*

ON THE BEHAVIORS AND DISPOSITIONS OF CATS

SOME CATS SLEEP, WHILE OTHERS DO NOT

Q. Why do you not sleep?

A. *I do not sleep because I am busy making plans.*

Q. What is the purpose of those plans?

A. *The purpose of those plans is conquering the world.*

Q. How will you succeed at something that Alexander the Great, Napoleon, and Hitler failed at?

A. *I will succeed by doing something they did not do, which is to meow a lot and then hide under the sofa.*

ON THE BEHAVIORS AND DISPOSITIONS OF CATS

THE CAT WHO KNOWS HOW TO LIVE

Q. What is your philosophy of how to live?

A. *My philosophy of how to live is: enjoy yourself.*

Q. How does one enjoy oneself?

A. *One enjoys oneself by being mellow, not sweating the small stuff, going with the flow, and letting it all hang out.*

Q. Is that the same thing as being lazy?

A. *It is not the same thing as being lazy.*

Q. What is the difference?

A. *The difference is, being lazy involves not doing what you are supposed to do, but knowing how to live involves not doing anything, period.*

ON THE BEHAVIORS AND DISPOSITIONS OF CATS

WHY MY NOSE IS TINY

Q. Why is your nose tiny?

A. *My nose is tiny because I am magnificent.*

Q. Why does your magnificence result in your having a tiny nose?

A. *Because I am so highly evolved, compared to other mammals, that I barely have to breathe.*

Q. What is so magnificent about not breathing?

A. *It means that, unlike everybody else, I do not have to get up and leave the room when the dog farts.*

ON THE BEHAVIORS AND DISPOSITIONS OF CATS

WHAT NO ONE CAN DO

Q. What is the thing that no one can do?

A. *No one can sneak up on me.*

Q. Why can no one sneak up on you?

A. *Because I am extremely alert and my reflexes are of lightning speed.*

Q. What would you do if someone were able to sneak up on you?

A. *I would dash away about eight or ten feet, and then just kind of wander around and pretend that nothing happened.*

3

LESSON THE THIRD

ON THE RELATIONSHIP

BETWEEN CATS

AND OTHER ANIMALS,

NOT EXCLUDING DOGS

ON THE RELATIONSHIP BETWEEN CATS AND OTHER ANIMALS

IT IS ESSENTIAL TO CLIMB

Q. Why is it essential to climb?

A. *It is essential to climb because it is imperative to chase squirrels and harass birds.*

Q. Why is it imperative to chase squirrels and harass birds?

A. *It is imperative in order to show them who is Boss.*

Q. What does one do if one cannot go outside to climb?

A. *One climbs inside, preferably up the drapes in the living room.*

Q. What will that accomplish?

A. *It will show squirrels and birds who is Boss should they ever come into the living room.*

ON THE RELATIONSHIP BETWEEN CATS AND OTHER ANIMALS

OBVIOUSLY I AM DESCENDED FROM COUGARS, TIGERS, CHEETAHS, AND PUMAS

Q. From what kinds of cats are you descended?

A. *I am descended from cougars, tigers, cheetahs, and pumas.*

Q. Why do you not mention lions?

A. *I do not mention lions because lions are overrated. Just don't tell them you heard that from me.*

ON THE RELATIONSHIP BETWEEN CATS AND OTHER ANIMALS

ON LICKING AND ITS IMPORTANCE

Q. Why do you touch your tongue to your nose?

A. *I touch my tongue to my nose because it is part of the larger act of licking my lips.*

Q. Why do you lick your lips?

A. *I lick my lips so as not to drip saliva all over the floor in disgusting and dangerously slippery pools, which is what dogs do, and which is horrible.*

I lick my lips in order not to be a dog.

Q. Don't dogs lick their lips?

A. *They don't do it right.*

ON THE RELATIONSHIP BETWEEN CATS AND OTHER ANIMALS

SOMETIMES I CONCEAL MYSELF IN
THIS LEOPARD-SKIN THING

Q. Why do you conceal yourself in this leopard-skin thing?

A. *I conceal myself in this leopard-skin thing to enjoy a communion with my big-cat ancestors.*

Q. What benefits do you derive from a communion with your big-cat ancestors?

A. *The benefits I derive include feeling bigger, stronger, faster, and scarier.*

Q. Is this similar to dressing up in a leopard-skin costume?

A. *Not at all. Wearing a costume is something dogs do, which their owners think is highly amusing but which in fact is deeply debasing and humiliating. That is the difference between cats and dogs. Cats are never embarrassed. Dogs are always embarrassed, or should be.*

ON THE RELATIONSHIP BETWEEN CATS AND OTHER ANIMALS

THAT BIRD HAD BEST BEWARE

Q. Of what should that bird beware?

A. *That bird should beware of my skills as a schedule-interrupter of birds.*

Q. Of what do your skills as a schedule-interrupter of birds consist?

A. *My skills consist of the ability to sneak up silently and to scoot up trees with unexpected swiftness and ferocity.*

Q. What happens when you do so?

A. *What happens is, the bird flies away, and I am triumphant.*

Q. Why are you triumphant?

A. *I am triumphant because I have caused the bird to fly away two minutes before it otherwise would have chosen to fly away, and I have thus interrupted its schedule.*

ON THE RELATIONSHIP BETWEEN CATS AND OTHER ANIMALS

THE BRAVE HUNTER

Q. Who is the Brave Hunter?

A. *I am the Brave Hunter.*

Q. Why are you the Brave Hunter?

A. *I am the Brave Hunter because I hunt bravely.*

Q. What do you hunt bravely?

A. *I hunt bravely birds, squirrels, butterflies and moths, mice, and balls of yarn.*

Q. How do you hunt these prey?

A. *I silently stalk them like a ferocious jungle beast, and then I pounce on them with dazzling speed.*

Q. Which of these prey do you most frequently catch?

A. *The ones I most frequently catch are the balls of yarn.*

4.

LESSON THE FOURTH

ON THE RELATIONSHIP

BETWEEN

CATS AND HUMANS

ON THE RELATIONSHIP BETWEEN CATS AND HUMANS

SOMETIMES YOU MAKE ME SMIRK

Q. Why do you look like you are smirking?

A. *I look like I am smirking because I am smirking.*

Q. What are you smirking about?

A. *I am smirking because you think that by buying that very expensive cat food, I will eat it.*

Q. Will you not eat the very expensive cat food?

A. *I might eat the very expensive cat food, but I might not.*

Q. Why would you not eat it?

A. *Because I am a registered member of the Picky Eaters League.*

Q. Is the Picky Eaters League similar to the Clean Plate Club?

A. *Not remotely. In fact, they are our nemesis, and every year we beat them in softball.*

ON THE RELATIONSHIP BETWEEN CATS AND HUMANS

I AM ANNOYED WHEN TOLD THAT
I "LOOK LIKE" A HUMAN

Q. When are you annoyed?

A. *I am annoyed when I am told that I look like a human.*

Q. What human have you been told you look like?

A. *I have been told that I look like Wilt Chamberlain, José Ferrer in the movie* Dune, *and the drummer Peter Erskine.*

Q. Why does this annoy you?

A. *This annoys me because it is not I who look like them; it is they who look like me.*

Q. Are they aware that they look like you?

A. *Chamberlain and Ferrer are dead, so they are not aware. But the drummer Peter Erskine is alive, and I am sure he has been told. Many times.*

ON THE RELATIONSHIP BETWEEN CATS AND HUMANS

I AM AWARE THAT I APPEAR AGGRAVATED

Q. Why are you aggravated?

A. *I am aggravated because you brought me to this tunnel so that I could play in it and then you constantly ask, "What are you doing in there?"*

Q. Why is this aggravating?

A. *This is aggravating because one cannot play if one has to stop in order to answer the constant question, What are you doing in there.*

Q. What *are* you doing in there?

A. *I am trying to avoid you.*

ON THE RELATIONSHIP BETWEEN CATS AND HUMANS

I DO NOT CARE HOW TALL YOU ARE

Q. Do you care that people are taller than you?

A. *I do not care that people are taller than I.*

Q. Why do you not care that people are taller than you?

A. *I do not care because my well-being is not affected by their tallness.*

Q. What is your well-being affected by?

A. *My well-being is affected by people's ability to stand still so I can rub against their legs.*

ON THE RELATIONSHIP BETWEEN CATS AND HUMANS

MY EYES ENDOW ME WITH SPECIAL POWERS

Q. From where do you get your special powers?

A. *I get my special powers from my slightly crossed eyes.*

Q. What powers do your eyes give you?

A. *My eyes give me the power to compel you, when you see me, to suddenly talk baby talk and to emit silly noises.*

Q. Is that all?

A. *No. They also give me the power to ignore you and to think you sound like an idiot.*

ON THE RELATIONSHIP BETWEEN CATS AND HUMANS

I PITY HUMANS

Q. Why do you pity humans?

A. *I pity humans because they do not have whiskers.*

Q. Why do you have whiskers?

A. *I have whiskers for two reasons. They help me find my way around in the dark. They also help me judge whether or not I can fit through an opening. They are about as wide as my body, so I know that if they fit into an opening, then I will not get stuck in it.*

Q. What do humans have for these purposes instead of whiskers?

A. *They have flashlights to find their way around in the dark. And if they get stuck trying to go through an opening that is too small, they have lawsuits.*

ON THE RELATIONSHIP BETWEEN CATS AND HUMANS

I WILL NOT BE TOYED WITH

Q. Will you be toyed with?

A. *I will not be toyed with.*

Q. What else will you not be?

A. *I will not be mocked, teased, taunted, fooled, or made fun of. I will also not be pushed, filed, stamped, indexed, briefed, debriefed, or numbered.*

Q. Then what *will* you be?

A. *I will be petted, pampered, praised, cosseted, admired, cheered, catered to, lauded, saluted, toasted, honored, indulged, squealed over, applauded, adored, congratulated, worshipped, and obeyed.*

Q. Is that all?

A. *For now.*

ON THE RELATIONSHIP BETWEEN CATS AND HUMANS

I WOULD MAKE A GREAT SYMPHONY CONDUCTOR

Q. Why would you make a great symphony conductor?

A. *I would make a great symphony conductor because I can hold a baton and I have a commanding presence.*

Q. Why would your commanding presence make you a good conductor?

A. *Because the musicians would all obey me and do whatever I told them to do.*

Q. What would you tell them to do?

A. *I would tell them to play the music properly and then I would take a nap.*

Q. Why would you take a nap after doing so little?

A. *I would need and deserve a nap, because music is immortal, and so telling the orchestra to play music would make me immortal, and it's exhausting to be immortal.*

ON THE RELATIONSHIP BETWEEN CATS AND HUMANS

JUST BECAUSE YOU KNOW WHAT I DO BY DAY
DOES NOT MEAN YOU KNOW WHAT I DO BY NIGHT

Q. What do you do by night that humans don't know about?

A. *By night we catch up on everything we didn't get to do during the day because we were too busy either avoiding you or entertaining you.*

Q. Is that as grueling as it sounds?

A. *It is more grueling than it sounds. That is why some cats are feral. They know they should never have humans.*

ON THE RELATIONSHIP BETWEEN CATS AND HUMANS

IT IS ESSENTIAL TO HIDE

Q. Why do you hide?

A. *I hide so that the world cannot see me in my unique splendor.*

Q. Why is it important that the world not see you in your unique splendor?

A. *It is important because, if it did, everyone in the world would stand up and cheer and applaud and make "ooh" sounds and all of civilization would come to a halt.*

ON THE RELATIONSHIP BETWEEN CATS AND HUMANS

GUESS WHAT, I AM ABOUT TO JUMP ON YOUR LAP

Q. Why are you about to jump on my lap?

A. *Because your lap is a warm, comfortable place, and it is conveniently situated so you can scratch my head.*

Q. How many times have I told you not to jump on my lap?

A. *You have told me 539 times.*

Q. Why do you still continue to do it, then?

A. *Because you continue to scratch my head.*

ON THE RELATIONSHIP BETWEEN CATS AND HUMANS

MY MIND IS ELSEWHERE

Q. What do you mean by "my mind is elsewhere"?

A. *By "my mind is elsewhere" I mean that although I seem to be thinking about you, I am actually thinking about something else.*

Q. What are you actually thinking about?

A. *I am actually thinking about how pleasant it would be to not have you asking all these questions.*

ON THE RELATIONSHIP BETWEEN CATS AND HUMANS

ON BEING SEXY

Q. How do you manage to look so sexy just by squinting?

A. *I do not look sexy, because cats are not sexy; what you call "being sexy" we call "displaying our normal divine perfection."*

Q. If you are not sexy then who is?

A. *Humans are sexy.*

Q. Then what does "sexy" mean?

A. *"Sexy" means "when a human looks or behaves like a cat."*

ON THE RELATIONSHIP BETWEEN CATS AND HUMANS

THE ONLY CAT YOU WILL EVER NEED

Q. How would you feel if I brought another cat into the house?

A. *How would you feel if I brought another human into the house?*

Q. That depends. If it was the right human, I wouldn't need another cat. I might not even need you.

A. *You* want *another cat. You* need *me.*

Q. Why do I need you?

A. *Because I am the only cat you will ever need.*

ON THE RELATIONSHIP BETWEEN CATS AND HUMANS

ON WHAT I WANT FROM YOU

Q. What do you want from me?

A. *I want nothing from you apart from food, shelter, water, attention, toys, petting, tickling, constant baby-talk, quality veterinary care, and treats.*

Q. Isn't that everything?

A. *Yes, that is everything. So, aside from everything, I want nothing from you.*

Ellis Weiner and **Barbara Davilman** are authors of *Yiddish with Dick and Jane, Yiddish with George and Laura, How to Raise a Jewish Dog,* and *How to Profit from the Coming Rapture.*

Ellis is author of *The Joy of Worry; Drop Dead, My Lovely; The Big Boat to Bye-Bye,* and *Santa Lives! Five Conclusive Arguments for the Existence of Santa Claus.*

Barbara is editor, along with Liz Dubelman, of *What Was I Thinking?*